From the Devotions

From the Devotions

POEMS BY

CARL PHILLIPS

GRAYWOLF PRESS

Publication of this volume is made possible in part by a
grant provided by the Minnesota State Arts Board through an
appropriation by the Minnesota State Legislature, and by a grant
from the National Endowment for the Arts. Significant support
has also been provided by Dayton's, Mervyn's, and Target
stores through the Dayton Hudson Foundation, the Andrew W.
Mellon Foundation, the McKnight Foundation, the General Mills
Foundation, the St. Paul Companies, and other generous
contributions from foundations, corporations, and individuals.
To these organizations and individuals who make our work
possible, we offer our heartfelt thanks.

Published by Graywolf Press
2402 University Avenue, Suite 203
Saint Paul, Minnesota 55114
All rights reserved.

www.graywolfpress.org

Published in the United States of America

ISBN 1-55597-263-2

Additional support for this publication
was provided by the Jerome Foundation.

2 4 6 8 9 7 5 3

Library of Congress Catalog Card Number: 97-70218

Cover art: Arthur G. Dove, "Shapes,"
The Phillips Collection, Washington, D.C.

Cover design by Jeanne Lee

Acknowledgments

Grateful acknowledgment is made to the editors of the following journals in which these poems first appeared:

AGNI: "From the Devotions"
Arion: A Journal of the Humanities and the Classics: "Renderings"
The Atlantic Monthly: "As from a Quiver of Arrows"
Boston Phoenix: "The Trees"
Boulevard: "In the Borghese Gardens," "Meditation:
   The Veil Between"
Callaloo: "Honey Hush," "Meditation: Perfection"
   (as "A Vanity of Wishes")
Delmar: "Alba: Come," "The Flume"
DoubleTake: "Luna Moth"
Harvard Review: "Alba: Failure," "Tunnel," "Two Versions
   of the Very Same Story"
The Marlboro Review: "Arcadia"
Muleteeth: "How We Met the Barbarians"
The Nebraska Review: "In the Days of Thrown Confetti"
The Paris Review: "On Morals"
Parnassus: Poetry in Review: "Meditation: Surrender"
Ploughshares: "Alba: Innocence," "The Blue Castrato"
Slate: "A Great Noise"
Solo: "Alba: After," "Meditation: The Dark Grotto," "The Hunters"
The Southwest Review: "On Restraint"
TriQuarterly: "No Kingdom," "The Sibyl"
The Yale Review: "The Full Acreage of Mourning"

"As from a Quiver of Arrows" also appeared in *The Best American Poetry 1996*, edited by Adrienne Rich and David Lehman, published by Scribner, 1996; and in *The Four Way Reader #2*, edited by Jane Brox, published by Four Way Books, 1996.

"As from a Quiver of Arrows," "From the Devotions," and "Tunnel" also appeared in the anthology *Things Shaped in Passing*, edited by Michael Klein and Richard McCann, published by Persea Books, 1997.

"The Gods" originally appeared as part of a prose memoir in the *James White Review* and in *Boys Like Us: Writers Tell Their Coming Out Stories*, edited by Patrick Merla, published by Avon, 1996.

For their patient reading and support of both the work and the worker, I thank Erin Belieu, Martha Collins, Doug Macomber, Fred Marchant, Fiona McCrae, Robert Pinsky, and Lloyd Schwartz.

for Doug

Contents

Therefore that he may raise the Lord throws down.

JOHN DONNE

The Living

The Trees

All night. From behind
curtain, turned suddenly all lifting
veil. From behind the screen behind that.

Their motion—their leaves' motion—
that of a torn wing,
that same unlovely

snagged flight, to the same half-tune
(your breathing)
to which the hours on blue

ankles parade as
down some questionable boulevard.
All night,

as if that other one (before
you, my body beside someone's but
not yet yours), when

"even the moon, even clouds"
were saying the trees that—as now,
then too—I was certain

could not know.
They think everything ends . . .
If so, then

why not this wake of losses (inevitable?
earned?)
that I have often enough come

so close to forgetting, I turn around
—and yes,
they are still with,

I think they will always be with—
no one is waving good-bye.
The trees

wave but, except to say "wind—
up again," this
means nothing. Sometimes,

we hold onto a life tightly.
Foolish; sad.
Not to know that it has already left us.

Alba: Innocence

Sunday. The bells, as expected. I cannot
help it if I rise, if finding the room too
fraught with light—all of it, the white
walls, the rinsed notion (always almost

inside then just out of reach) of God, your
body gleaming in sleep where the sun falls
on it and away from, falls on and away—
I have to shut my one good eye and at once

the leaves falling but now blurred make it
possible to see how it happens, a bruise
lifting itself over time from the darker
blues to, slowly, something like amber,

to at last whatever, before the wounding,
the flesh was. Imagining the flesh before
or without knowledge, I want to say it is
most like song untrained, whose beauty,

when it occurs, surprises even itself—
but isn't it also, more commonly, just
meat, or isn't it good soil waiting, that
does not, cannot know that it is waiting?

Therefore, it is innocence. Therefore,
a capacity for suffering more vast, even,
than the landscape whose particulars, you
remember, we drove past, the red of sunset

upon them: the bull in mid-lumbering over
the cow (still with patience, with fear?),
almost, not yet inside her; the sudden
bursting of crows, all cinders flying over

where once, presumably, was some small life.
We were tired, hungry, faintly hungry for
each other. We kept driving: east, home,
toward a dark we couldn't fast enough get to.

Luna Moth

No eye that sees could fail to remark you:
like any leaf the rain leaves fixed to and
flat against the barn's gray shingle. But

what leaf, this time of year, is so pale,
the pale of leaves when they've lost just
enough green to become the green that *means*

loss and more loss, approaching? Give up
the flesh enough times, and whatever is lost
gets forgotten: that was the thought that I

woke to, those words in my head. I rose,
I did not dress, I left no particular body
sleeping and, stepping into the hour, I saw

you, strange sign, at once transparent and
impossible to entirely see through, and how
still: the still of being unmoved, and then

the still of no longer being able to be
moved. If I think of a heart, his, as I've
found it. . . . If I think of, increasingly, my

own. . . . If I look at you now, as from above,
and see the diva when she is caught in mid-
triumph, arms half-raised, the body as if

set at last free of the green sheath that has—
how many nights?—held her, it is not
without remembering another I once saw:

like you, except that something, a bird, some
wild and necessary hunger, had gotten to it;
and like the diva, but now broken, splayed

and torn, the green torn piecemeal from her.
I remember the hands, and—how small they
seemed, bringing the small ripped thing to me.

Honey Hush

I.

It will be as if: fur. As if trust
could be fur. Imagine,
bees coat the sugar body

that is yours . . .
see how your body hums?
Say you love them. Now. You must

say you love them. And I would, and
—I would, until it was true
almost, and then true:

I could love the bees,
and neither mind nor be surprised
by their weight, slow as drones

and as deliberate, upon me.

II.

Every fall, still, the deer swim the cold channel
between the island whose name I don't know
and this island.

Their instinct is: they need more; and that, here,
they will find it. From the shore, children
make of their small hands small binoculars,

and guess at which ones will drown.
For some of the deer always drown.
They lose, I think, whatever for a deer

hope can be. And it weighs something,
that loss. How else understand it,
this swimmer, that one, there and then

not, except as when sometimes the body
meets a weight sudden, unlooked-for,
and large, the way persuasion is large—

or despair: no struggle attends that descent.

Arcadia

I. Desire

The horse does not drink, but I am sure
he is wanting.

             Dappled neither in shadow
nor sun, his body.

               His body like mine,
in places: what would, but does not.

Minding the grass, how it crumples easy—
gentle, bring him to me.

II. He Is a Lover of Horses

He is a lover of horses, but a troubled child also.
He does not know the difference between the smell
of his body and the sweet hay it has always been
his one job to carry. He does not know the difference
between horses and men. He gives the men his sweet
body—to the horses, the hay. Sometimes, it is
hay he gives the men, and then a grief that he knows,
when they leave him. The horses are different.
They take their tongues to his body—for its salt,
for its sweetness. What he feels—
it isn't grief; it isn't love, and not hunger.
It has a name, he tells the men, when they call him.

III. A Late and Solitary Figure

Thunder, and lightning. He keeps his head down,
between his legs, that are not thunder, and lightning.
The one hand down his pants is not—however
mathematic—a proof, but feels good. The rain
the storm has brought with it, as it falls down his back,
this also feels good, but proves nothing proves: nothing.
The field that contains him is a wide one, and endless,
though this is not the whole world, it's only now
that he thinks so. He is sure he is the one flower in it.

IV. The Taming

He is not like the others, who say nothing and leave
soon. This one—done, but still stiff—is a dark
weight upon him, that stays, groaning/whispering
baby and *pie*. It is neither of these, though, that
the boy feels inside. He feels a blinding that is—
strange, and not before that he remembers—less a
pain than a light that won't stop, going through him.
He thinks: *the sun maybe, maybe buried inside me.*
Why else this heat, and this dark, all around? But
if he opened his eyes now, he'd see the sun there
without him and, beneath it, the same horses—some
making for shade, others there already, kneeling down
in the cool grass. He would notice their bodies: not
silk and not water. To look at, unbroken, clean. His.

In the Days of Thrown Confetti

You remember.
Back when, I suppose,
it could be said we didn't care

about the earth, anymore
than about the flesh, but I
don't say it.

We cared.
In that way that is
the best way, half-heedless,

reckless. It meant
we believed: *good lasts,*
good luck is a thing rampant.

Now, as if luck were some
mercurial field to be
sown, we throw seed. Or

we throw the rice that finally
lands here, on this city
pavement, as if

the point were to summon
proof—in the form of birds
gray, mottled,

and not particularly
clean—of our best wishes.
In the days of thrown confetti,

part of the point
was the birds:
that they should come;

that they should be,
on purpose,
disappointed.

When they rose,
they carried with them,
took someplace else their hunger.

In the Borghese Gardens

The sad Roman emperors were not the many
who had themselves declared gods,
but the others,
the few who really believed it.

It is the same thing, you tell me, *with love.*

How every once in a while,
when a man of small frame feeds the birds,
or loves flowers,

He is crazy, we say, bored;
or we are bored, and we say *Look,*
there's a saint, and move on.

We keep walking because the park
is still lovely,
the swans are,
the hungry way they tear at their food

like it's history, or the heart, and not bread.

No Kingdom

So little wakes you—why
should a little rain,
or my leaving

to stand under it
and naked
because I can,

all neighbors down,
at last down,
for the dreaming, and

every wasp—daily, the yard's
plague—gone,
returned to

whatever shingle or board
roofs their now
thrumless heliport.

Tremblefoot,
mumbler,
you've left

your glass on the porch-railing
—neglect, as
what is fragile, seen

through,
but not at this hour empty:
the way disease does

the body, the way desire
can, or how God
is said to,

slowly rain fills the glass.
Never mind
that no kingdom was ever won

by small gestures:
I'm tipping the rainwater out.
The glass I'll put

here, where you'll find it.

Alba: Failure

If the bare trees at the glass were kings
really, I would know they bend over in grief,
mourning their lost brilliant crowns that

they can only watch, not reach as, beneath them,
they let go of all color all flash all sway,
it would be better, I wouldn't have to say *no*

they are not kings, they are trees, I know this,
and if they bend it is wind only, it is nature,
isn't it also indifference? Passing yesterday

the bodies that, wrapped and wrapped, lay
sprawled above the steam as it left the vents
of my city, I could only fumble for the words

(*dead lamb, dead lamb*) to some song to sing
parts of, I gave, but what I gave—is it
right to say it helped no one, or can I say

I brought lullaby, sealed a thin life,
awhile longer, in sleep? What is failure?
Having read how there were such things as

orchard lamps for keeping the good fruit, on
colder nights, from freezing, I was curious
for that kind of heat go the lines from

a poem I never finished. The shorter version
is: once, twice, in a difficult time, I have
failed you. No poetry corrects this. But

does it mean we don't love? In the last poem
of you waking, I am any small bird, unnoticed,
above, watching; you are the traveler who

can't know (there is fog, or no stars, a steep
dark) that the all but given up for impossible
next town is soon, soon. Come. We turn here.

Gods Various

The Blue Castrato

I. To His Savior in Christ

If I did not, as I do, know well
to love you first, I'd love my voice
instead, cause you to yield the throne
whose impossibly precious batting I
could sing all day and never start
to know—it is blasphemy or worse
even to think it (*Domine, me—*
ut placet—me retine). I'd love
my voice that is all I need to know
of a clean, a clear, that I am promised
will never leave me, even should
I want it. Who could want it? Even
in this your difficult field, your vale,
I sing—and see? The grasses open.

II. To His Diary

Played Mister Lazy, mostly. Found
the weather fine, but did not step
inside it. Prayed, as usual. Read
the new books that, if I don't watch out,
I shall find myself fairly whelmed
by. Over soup, had wrongful thoughts—
only of wanting something like more
variety, but bad is bad:
said prayer again. Restored, I glued
the handle back on the broken pot
I've never loved: no color, badly
fired. Though it looks more humble now,
I like it more. . . . The evening quiet.
Some hunger (food, et al.). Resisted.

III. To His Right Hand

Soft!—Is it you? Idiot. Who's
expected? Huh? But his body . . . I can't
forget it, no. Yes, I can:
don't want to. Still—how easy it is,
remembering, then not, and then
not minding, it's that forgotten. Smell
the bay tree's leaves again, lie down
where it happened, fill the mouth with what
comes closest, the whole time touching
flesh as if flesh were wood, as if luck
could be somehow coaxed from hiding, into
your hand—O dry, and empty. Must
stop wanting. Or less. More sleep. But *how?*,
as usual. I'm better than this. I am.

IV. To His Psychiatrist

Volcano. No, a bud that brooks
no forcing. No. No, now I see
it: my heart. I mean to save it. Here's
Falsetto Childhood; here, bewigged,
is Ardor, antoinetting hot
among a herd that bellows, bleeds.
Here is the pool I spoke of. Dark
is the water, but step up (here, take care)
to the edge: the water clears, is good.
The bulls want only to drink, to cool
what burns, but the water itself is hot.
Steam, then the dream ends. Ends the same:
same fish, marked *help*, swims belly-up
my way. Plays horn. Spits up:—a lily.

V. To His Savior in Christ

Haven't I hymned your praise enough?
What I would not, given the choice, have given,
I gave: my voice is token. For you—
for years, what made for a life—I sang,
I have caused entire crowds to cry
out to you *Uncle*; as pigeons to home,
they sought and came to a kind of resting
upon your deep/your fair/your not-
to-be-understood-in-this-our-life-
time breast. Forgive me if I say
I'm sometimes sorry. I've licked the broad
tracks that your grace leaves after; sweet?
If I say I've found, known sometimes sweeter,
I'm no less yours. In need, Your Servant.

VI. *To His Body at 42 (A Valentine)*

Dear Vessel—Little Boat—of Me:
how lovely (still!) you are, resting
on water, you can't know. You know
no field, but drift toward one: there,
each blade of grass wears well its jacket
of dew my lord Dusk provides—I know,
I tasted, watched each one, formal, bend
then straighten . . . years ago. . . . Surely
as songdom's Jesus loves you—yes,
I love you too. I wish you sails
of whatever is proof against storm
and what else tears. I wish you fanfare:
cymbals, and flutes; despite a life,
these still-immaculate-sounding notes.

On Morals

Naturally, the preference is for
victory, not persistence—
which, like fire if not put out,
in time will burn itself out.

Mere watching is not, of course,
particularly victory, but it need not,
either, signify perversion.
One tends increasingly to think

on one's first flasher in the park,
that first uncircumcised, ungainly
cock—how, as when some trick is
near, not to watch was the impossible

thing, waiting for what the pulled
bandanna, what the dove might next
turn into—and to feel guilty, as
if Lucretius had never written of joy

attendant, too, upon the witnessing
of violence, horror, any shame
when it falls on those not ourselves.
It is part of the nature of things

that from the grafting of distance
upon failure comes a pleasure for which,
sadly, one is more and more meant
to feel compelled to seek forgiveness—

which last, if it occurs at all,
generally does so at that angle
at which the sun has never, in fact,
risen. That is, it appears to.

Renderings

(Seventh century B.C.)

Sappho

Need, desire:
that which we must have,
the other, that we want to;

what do they know,
who haven't learned
the two can be the same thing?

Eventually,
it ends, it does,
so they say—

strangers, all of them,
to you, fair
Aphrodite.

They have not touched
your hand,
and burned from it,

or heard the beating
of your sparrows, drawing
near—known that terror.

They have not met your son.

Archilochus

By the spear, let's call it,
came my life
of bread and of good wine, once.
Leaning on it, I could put away thirst.

Dear friend,
you remember.

True Desire—that boy,
that loosener of limbs—
had not yet undone mine.

Anonymous

The yellow, once-noisy
wrestling grounds of the palaestra
are empty.

Soon the enslaved will come
to rake smooth again
the oil- and sun-hardened sand.

All the men have gone elsewhere,
to eat, to find rest,
their tired bodies flung wherever

there is shade,
in this season of heat and the Dog Star.

By evening, their strength restored,
there will be other games than this one.

Anacreon

Madness, in all forms,
every kind of confusion:
these are sometimes the playthings
of Eros.
      Sometimes, a hammer—

as when once, like a blacksmith,
he struck me, shaped me,
then dipped my body
in the winter-cold flood-tide
of longing.

Mimnermus

What is life or anything sweet
inside it, to one removed
from Aphrodite, more
precious than gold?

The secret, heat-soothing gifts
of desire,
the bed
and what goes on there,
whatever flowers of pleasure there are
worth snatching—to men, women,
both—

When these have gone and, having gone,
no longer matter to me—
then, too, let go my body.

Anacreon

You,
a boy,
but shooting glances like girls,

it's not that I don't seek from you
more;
you don't listen.

It isn't right.

Whatever I do with my body,
my soul, at least,
is no racehorse.

However lovely,
and skilled with your hands,
you are no charioteer.

From an Epitaph

Stranger, stopping to read this,
know that I was an artist.
I believed in the gods
but especially in two,
whose signs—whenever
they gave them—
I never failed to see.
None of this, in the end,
could save me.

The Hunters

That they, in fitful bands, came
and were immediately dismayed: a prairie, no gazelles,

only bees, the usual colored-in flowers.
Were dismayed and—all blond, all bow astrain, all

arrow—were foolish in
the manner of Beauty when it has fumbled a good ball:

aloud, the stadium groans, cries *Alas, alas, all is
undone*; or were foolish in the manner of

Beauty when it has fumbled a good ball:
the dance stops, the hall fills with *A rogue, a rogue,*

here is no lord.
That it was that hour when there is light still, and

still there are bees, but also—
as where marjoram must invisibly, unmistakably grow

(a scent, rising)—thoughts of hunger, home.
So that many were most desperate and—poker-faced,

clearly admiring no empty hand, and
no gazelles or other fair game forthcoming—some fell

to capturing the bees, with hands that
accordingly, full of victory, swelled as if pretending

a proud chest, or a heart;
others tore at the flowers. That their beauty was as

various as flowers: the one
stringing his bow; another, the way he had raised his.

On Restraint

I.
One could do worse than to begin
with the martingale, that elaborate
leather-passed-between-the-forelegs device

whose purpose is to allow the rider some
control over the horse's natural desire
to look occasionally upward, or away.

One could consider its effectiveness
now: horseless, idly tossed into
a bed of what appears to be

—yes, they are wild strawberries;
the fruit, in disregard
of the sweat-worn leather, coming

ripe even as one kneels down
to take it; the leaves that don't just
for rings and straps stop growing.

II.
There are horses in the distance, so say so.

There are horses in the distance,
not running, smoke-still.

Not running yet: the idea of *To run.*

Not running but getting ready to run.

There are no horses in the distance, but
say so.

There is smoke,

or a fog that, from this distance,
is any number of horses, not running.

III.

Weary of extravagance, one remembers with
fondness some painting in which the artist
had not forgotten how to strike a right

balance between decorum and pain: yes,
to the captive's each arm and leg is
attached a thick rope, at the other end

of which is a horse upon which, in turn,
sits a rider whose task it will be to
make the horse bolt forward. But all

in due time. The artist has left the ropes
slack, the horses look out at random—sky,
grass, the large crowd. The captive's face

is tastefully obscured by smoke from a pipe
the captain is only waiting to finish
before giving the four horsemen their signal.

IV.

The saddle sits on the table that would be
—otherwise, without saddle—bare.

(The sun does not count.)

(The dust doesn't, sunlit or not.)

The saddle sits on the table and every song
is a blue one:

Than the saddle, riderless,
and itching no steed, tell me
what is more lonely?

Do not sing it.

Regard instead the saddle, its silence.

V.
The habit of riding bareback is a habit
one prefers not to recall having taken
some part in, even if only the one time,

but one is human, and remembers the slow
to slowish canter that was like—
love, beginning. And the progression,

going at first unnoticed, toward gallop:
permission? or the horse itself taking
charge, until the rider was thrown?

Although one suspects that everything
inclines toward release, one would like
not to think it. One would like nothing

more than to forget it all: how beautiful
he was then, like a man, not a horse.
—But very like a horse, how he ran.

How We Met the Barbarians

We knew by the boots,
gone from restive to still
in the courtyard,

that our walls had been taken,
but that didn't stop us
from refreshing the sheets

at the window, and leaning,
as we always had, nude and
just-showered, against them,

we were that moved
by the light falling
like nothing but light

off the weapons
that wearily slung
and unslung themselves

from the enemy's shoulders;
that eager to know, too,
what happens, what

becomes of a grace,
already hammered thin
to breaking by siege

and hard custom, in
the calloused and
stiff palms of defeat:

any moment, we thought,
that sound akin to
desire we'd heard

history makes—
one life folding
into another.

Alba: After

So you were spared.
So you didn't run for your small life but
instead, impatient with disaster's slow coming,
drove toward it.
And there has since been
my weight beneath yours,
the unremarkable, safe passing through
dream, after, and now
morning, the light
routinely finding each window.
The trees. Birds.
There is an hour, the poet said, when
the boat's only safety lies in letting it lie
to, moored among whatever brush bank
or shore offers.
What is meant by the boat?
The body?
The life not yet lost, despite the many losses
life also is?
Where is the brush that will mean rescue?
Love, there is little good
that can't, too, turn bad. For this, let us
be thankful.
For the violence pitching
its taut way toward a resolve
that sometimes can only be,
can't it, smash.
For there being nothing then,
not even the knowing how much we stand to lose
by it, that can keep us from that beauty.

The Gods

It is not that they don't exist but that they are
everywhere disguised, that no one space than another

is less fit or more likely:
the lighthouse, tower of bright, distant witness;

the same dull bird as before, still extendedly calling
where has every wing flown

—the sand, the salt grass.
Think of any of those times that they are said

to have assumed the slowing burden of flesh
and done damage; recall Christ, then (all over)

the boy you found lying restive
(among the sand, the salt grass),

naked—save for the words **breakfast included**
lipsticked onto his chest in thick, plum letters;

and that particular beauty that disarms first,
then attracts

(in which way he most resembled any bad road
collision from which the bodies have not yet been

freed, he resembled the bodies).
They are to any of our hungers as, once, the water was

to that Portuguese man-of-war that you can see
is collapsed now, stranded, useless to itself

against any mouth toward it and open.
They were equally to do with your saying *no*

and your saying *no* not because of not wanting but
Because, you thought, *what else can it be, so much*

wanting, except wrong? Their forgiveness
has never been to be sought: it will, or will not

befall us—you are not stupid, you know this.
As you have known, always, their favor: that it is

specific and can be difficult to see, it is that thin
and that clean. Easily it breaks, and it breaks clean.

The Sibyl

the way down is easy   Aeneid VI

I.
Crossroads vision,
medallion,
wet star;

bull to my steer;
to my bell,
steady clapper,

the rope
and, inside the wind's
sleeve, that

arm that pulls and
pulls it:
by these and other

names was I told I
should call to the god;
and he—

I was what?
a mere girl? And
already: chosen.

II.
I saw what desperate
is, what also
is faith:

gold bullion, some
lord's staff or
cloak—stiff,

precious; steam off
beautiful beasts
cut freshly down;

and those little
sacrificial
cakes, those

stand-ins
for flesh,
as if it were

that simple:
some honey,
some ground meal.

III.
Have you ever
seen them,
the bodies

of the all but
drowned, all
blear, and ash?

Then a turn—
whatever soul,
flame, life

inside deciding
yes, it will stay.
And here come

the other colors,
making their
slow, defeated

way back: say what
that is, that
causes. He was that.

IV.
To bidding not
mine would he come
and fill me with

himself, so full
I must, against
bursting, open

finally my
mouth. Each
word was his.

As my body was
also so much his
that it almost

escaped him,
the small
and smaller

part that was
still myself.
And I refused him.

V.
No damage.
No blame. Instead,
I was to name any

gift. *As many as*
are the grains
of sand one hand

might hold, so many
years let me live.
When he left—

nothing different
at first. On
the floor, the usual

clatter of leaves:
brown, cracked with
age, the weight of

prophecy upon them.
I looked at my hands.
Then the leaves.

VI.
There is a third
gate, neither
ivory, nor horn:

the flesh, what
cannot help but
fail, come bone,

come shine. What
is history to myth?
Not the tree whose

leafless branches
make a crown within
which, this morning,

nine birds sing—
but the birds, that
take as done, as

granted, all that sky,
his mouth, blue hole
I am falling through.

The Veil Between

A Great Noise

Then he died.
And they said: *Another soul free.*

Which was the wrong way to see it, I thought,
having been there,
having lain down beside him until

his body became rigid with what I believe
was not the stiffening of death
but of surprise, the initial
unbelief of the suddenly ex-slave hearing
Rest; let it fall now, this burden.

The proof most commonly put forth for the soul
as a thing that exists and weighs
something is that
the body weighs something less, after death—

a clean fact.

In *The Miraculous Translation of the Body
of Saint Catherine of Alexandria to Sinai,*
the number of angels required to bear the body
all that way through the air
comes to four,

which tells us nothing
about weight, or the lack of it, since
the angels depicted
are clearly those for whom

the only business is hard labor,

the work angels,
you can tell:
the musculature;
the resigned way they wear clothes.

Beyond them in rank,
in the actual presence of God,
the seraphim stand naked, ever-burning,

six-winged: two to fly with,
in back; two at the face to withstand
the impossible winds that
are God;

and a third pair—for modesty,
for the covering
of sex.

A great
noise is said to always
attend them:
less the humming of wings than
the grinding you'd expect

from the hitching of what is hot,
destructive,
and all devotion

to the highest, brightest star.

Alba: Come

—as he did. Then
go down to the water, to where
he finally closed his slit of mouth,
and died, the world distancing,
more distant, gone. Don't forget
there were two, the one who died,
and the one who made him, whose
feet as they approached, rising
from and drowning among the dry
prone-to-crack leaves, must have
—as yours are now—been also birds
flushed from their cover and brought
abruptly down. His feet like that,
his mouth like any mouth when it opens
to say *You want, I'll suck you off*:
not like threat, but offering; a gift.

The rest—This is the light as it
found him. Take it. Put it on.
This of course is not the exact
same light, but the same moon
appearing to leave, the same sun
appearing. This is the light, this
is the way he was found inside it:
naked, not counting the small
rain all over, not counting the blood
that still, despite rain, glazed
his chest, the blood coming
from what—severed and lifted
from its nest—the hand did not
so much hold anymore as wear,
Egyptian, the scarab worn in death,
the guarantee, safe passage away.

The Flume

The idea is to pretend
that it is real,
the hollowed log we

step into, and
not plastic;
that its passage

is random, to do with
current and wind only,
we are to forget

what we know or have
heard of motors
distantly, invisibly

handled, let go all
suspicion of planned
slants and turns to this

channel, narrow,
fiberglass, sectioned,
painted green to seem

verdant, and indeed
as we approximate
swiftness, the effect

is almost banks
overgrown. We are
perhaps meant

to recall Cooper's
slayer of deer, or to
think Lewis and Clark

could, in fact, be
the two men in the log
just before ours

—and they can be,
if we ignore that
the one man does not

merely look as if he
is dying: he really is;
and however often

some may look then
look away from
the other man straddling

the crossbar behind,
his knees half-framing,
half-bracing the man

in front, the two men
are lovers and like us,
in coming here, mean

too, if only briefly,
to come away
from something else.

And briefly,
it is easy, as we are
carried—jostling,

not jostling—to parts
especially protected
by trees, the sun

rare as light
in those paintings
depicting America as lush,

virgin, generally
benighted except at
the one corner

where two men—
are they settlers,
explorers?—stand

dwarfed but not daunted
by the wild around them:
they have found

or they have been found by
the one pocket of light,
so impossible that

Surely, they believe,
It is God and it is
Eden—

for a moment,
it is like that:
leaves, leaves,

the birds are made again
stupid and do not think
to regard us. Then

what has passed for
some time as the land
opens up, and we are

borne severally,
unnaturally, via pulley,
up in preparation to

descend the flume proper,
this ride that, as
it turns out, is no

different in purpose
from the others:
to risk almost-death,

to die nearly—
yes, terror, yes
resistance,

but as well an emptying
of laughter as of
stones from the body and,

never far, the knowing
that it will end
soon, we can somewhere

find food, another ride,
any other and next
thing. For who can

not want to? Who among us
is not now suddenly,
and beautifully,

ravenous?—even,
perhaps especially
the man who, we have

almost forgotten,
is dying but now,
remembering, we want and

don't want to say is
as we are, not any less
long for this world.

Two Versions of the Very Same Story

after Borges

I.

In Ravenna, Dante's dying. He's alone,
unjustified—so, any man. Except
he's gotten this dream from God, from Heaven, thrown
straight in his withered lap. Said God: *You've wept
at all of it—life, labor—all a waste.
But know behind it all, my purpose went,
unknown to you: now hear it.* Then God graced
the poet, as with a crown, with His intent.
When Dante heard, he blessed his bitter days,
but now, awake, he wonders why it is
that, having learned at last the complex ways
in which the world's machinery works, what's his
or briefly was seems not his anymore.
Ravenna. Dante dying. Like before.

II.

The leopard cannot understand the dream.
How God said: *Where you live, you'll die—a cage
where, one day, a man will see you. You won't seem,
to him, forgettable. He'll take a page
and cast you there, a word, but more than word,
a symbol in a poem. For this you live
imprisoned, as you'll die.* The leopard heard
and, hearing, understood. What God would give
the leopard took, and gladly. That was then.
But now, awake, he's still (but doesn't, can
not know) a beast, craves love, what's cruel, to rend
the flesh, smell, taste the steam—so, any man:
caged not in dawn or dusk—between the two;
where floorboards, bars don't change. The people do.

Tunnel

Come now, if ever.
When it is raining this gentle
and the first thought is of semen,
and the second thought is of lilies
when by their own pale weight
they bend, sing to the ground something,
and the third thought is of
what joy or sadness can be
available to what is finally a lily
and can't sing.

:

And you said *It is wind* and *It is heat,*
hearing the doors shift in their frames.
Because you could not say what also
to call it: God as what is relentless,
God as oil, redolent, proffered;
the final, necessary cross-stitch of
death whose meaning is that everything
finds closure; or the meaningless,
already tipped, disembodied scales
in which we are all of us, inescapably,
found wanting, because how can we
not want?

:

—In the street below, the latest version of cool need, his
   black car shining in such a way as to make all of it (that
   any children around follow, that each longs to see his own
   face given back, and the one boy, that he is chosen, is
   getting in) seem natural, inevitable.

:

the body, bright thing and holy   *the body as raft-like*
the ocean beneath it as waves   *the waves as many small fans*
the one you loved, he is dead   *the one I love, he is dead*
each wave beneath him is blue   *—blue, collapsing*

:

—Sunday morning, the Greek diner. The men in pairs from
last night. Again the different, more difficult
tenderness that is two men with only their briefly shared
flesh in common as they eat and don't eat much, together.
At the window *brush/fail, brush/fail* go the leaves.

:

After Patroklos, impatient, took the armor of Achilles,
after he put it on his own body
and rode into battle, and then died,
Achilles fell into grief—
not for the loss of the armor that was his,
but for love of the man who had last worn it,
who could never, now,
be brought back.
His goddess-mother, Thetis, hearing
as far away as the sea's floor
his uncontrollable cries, hurried to him.
A lot of words, armor, a new shield . . .

:

Here is the sun.
Take some.
Here is the rain, in no apparent way
holy, but serving still.
Wash.
Drink.
Here is the body.
Do not imagine now balm.
The wounds are to be
left open.

for Frank

As from a Quiver of Arrows

What do we do with the body, do we
burn it, do we set it in dirt or in
stone, do we wrap it in balm, honey,
oil, and then gauze and tip it onto
and trust it to a raft and to water?

What will happen to the memory of his
body, if one of us doesn't hurry now
and write it down fast? Will it be
salt or late light that it melts like?
Floss, rubber gloves, a chewed cap

to a pen elsewhere—how are we to
regard his effects, do we throw them
or use them away, do we say they are
relics and so treat them like relics?
Does his soiled linen count? If so,

would we be wrong then, to wash it?
There are no instructions whether it
should go to where are those with no
linen, or whether by night we should
memorially wear it ourselves, by day

reflect upon it folded, shelved, empty.
Here, on the floor behind his bed is
a bent photo—why? Were the two of
them lovers? Does it mean, where we
found it, that he forgot it or lost it

or intended a safekeeping? Should we
attempt to make contact? What if this
other man too is dead? Or alive, but
doesn't want to remember, is human?
Is it okay to be human, and fall away

from oblation and memory, if we forget,
and can't sometimes help it and sometimes
it is all that we want? How long, in
dawns or new cocks, does that take?
What if it is rest and nothing else that

we want? Is it a findable thing, small?
In what hole is it hidden? Is it, maybe,
a country? Will a guide be required who
will say to us how? Do we fly? Do we
swim? What will I do now, with my hands?

The Full Acreage of Mourning

The truth is, *I was at the point of utter ruin.*
Alone. The one tree at last no plum tree, but
purple, like plums. And all day in the leaves
the little nameless Solomon birds saying who:

Who has woe? Who has sorrow? Who has wounds
without cause? I am no stranger to wisdom—
Like a sparrow in its flitting Like a swallow
in its flying Like a lame man's legs Like a

thorn that goes up into the hand Like an archer
who wounds everybody is love, yes, I know that,
there are books and I have read them, there
are flowers, the ones whose streaks spell out

beautifully "alas!", all the others marked *You*
will be like one who lies down in the midst
of the sea or *like one who lies on the top of*
a mast in fine print: of each one haven't I

taken to my mouth the thin petal and swallowed?
The truest words are something else at any
given moment can happen, will, has happened.
I could say that *at the window of my house I*

looked out through my lattice, and I perceived
among the youths a young man spitting proverbs
like "You can lead, if it is thirsty, any horse
to the water," and that would be but one version.

Another is: Unable to forget, I sought out every
space that I thought might contain you. Each
one I entered. At each I called Come, or Where
now, Little Shield, or Little Sir Refuge, here?

Meditation:

The Veil Between

That is, they with their backs to us, they with their hands
holding nothing, no mirror to see by, no one good cure.
Us then ourselves with none of our ills in great measure
bettered—still straits desperate and perilously
narrow, births especially dubious, mice, moles, false
witness, the chills, trouble of foot, ruptures bodily and
spiritual, doubt, palpitations, storm, stiffness of neck,
of heart, overly troublesome birds in too great abundance,
death sudden or too slow, quarreling, swine both real and
only seeming to be so, bruises, losing what we want most
not to, mad dogs, luck that is bad, visual soreness, shame
and the hands—because of it—folded, likewise flood
and nowhere a raft to sail on. And they not sad, apparently,
and not particularly waving. And just the wind for a sound:
cold, hollow. Us calling it song or saying *No, it is grace.*

Perfection

To take everything back, reverse the limbs turned out
outrageous, the breath foundering. To wake from

where flesh—like every other road there—was
hard, lasting. And find it dream—and the dreaming,

enough. To rise full from the long table
of example: the double stags, gutted, skinned, dressed—

all that meat, at last, rendered useful;
the upturned brace of pheasant, still struggling, still

knowing dimly, more dimly, darkly the gamekeeper's
kid-hugged fist. To lie naked, down, and

squired, to either side a lord gone stiff and restive
in full court dress. To steer, on sootless,

drama-less wings those undeeded acres between seduce
and persuade. O never to get, nor have

got there. To thirst gothically, to want—
like a spire: no discernible object but more sky.

The River Road

That certain birds—
the eagle, in whom come together in
something like marriage rapaciousness, grace;
or, rapacious too and stuffed with grace,
all manner of falcon, also of hawk each
kind—suggested the archangels:
this makes sense.

And the sky meaning,
more nakedly than usual, only the usual
(try, you will never match it, this blue),
the river widening to reflect so much more
of the same—and weren't you hungry,
besides?—how difficult was it, just
then, to see God?

But that stretch of
flat barges on hold, each awaiting the one
sign: *Come, the water lies clear*; how, bored,
you turned away toward the chalk, no, chalk-
colored bluffs that all day had been there
but now, regarded, looked
athletic, fallen—

Confess,
it has surprised you, thus to understand the soul.

Surrender

As when,
into the canyon that means,
whose name—translated—
means *Without Measure, Sorrow*

from the hand that,
for so long, has meant
give,
but now—broken—gives in,

is released
the garland   /swag   /bouquet
(that—look,
look again—means

only as much as what it is:
eucalyptus,
kangaroo's paw,
the grass called eel),

that he, impossibly, might catch it.

The Dark Grotto

If he is disease, he is also
any wanting and more wanting
of something, he is snow. *All of these.*

Like snow, how it embraces,
becomes at first its object,
how it seems to become and
then swallows its object. *All these.*

As if the body were dependent
on outposts; and the nightwatch
—slain, asleep, drunk, or
worse, bored, unregarding: *Himself, all of these.*

Whose breast was sky-endless
and redolent of—almond?
an almond tree burning? having
already burnt, just after? *Yea, these.*

In whose lap lay the wound
not invisibly bleeding, but
the blood suggesting other
than blood: *rose, hard token, these?*

And seeing, I knew the eye:
and then I knew nothing.
And tasting, I knew the tongue:

Isaiah

Who are these that fly   like cloud
      Enter into the rock
      and hide in the dust

· ·

An antelope in a net
The cup of staggering
      Is there not a lie in my right hand

· ·

The timbrel   breathless   falls toward song
      We moan and moan
      like doves

· ·

The oil of gladness instead
      of mourning
The mantle of praise instead of   a faint spirit

· ·

      Go
and fall backward
All flesh is grass   The grass withers

· ·

The grass
shall become reeds
      And be broken   And rushes   And snared

From the Devotions

I.

As if somewhere, away, a door had slammed shut.
—But not metal; not wood.

Or as when something is later remembered only
as something dark in the dream:

torn, bruised, dream-slow
descending, it could be anything—

tiling, clouds,
you again, beautifully consistent, in no

usual or masterable way   *leaves, a woman's*
shaken-loose throat, shattered

eyes of the seer, palms, ashes, the flesh
instructing; you, silent.

A sky, a sea requires crossing and, like that,
there is a boat or, like that, a plane:

for whom is it this way now, when
as if still did I lie down beside, still

turn to, touch
                    I can't, I could not save you?

II.

Not, despite what you believed, that
all travel necessarily ends here, at the sea.

I am back, but only because.
As the sun only happens to meet the water

in such a way that the water becomes
a kind of cuirass: how each piece takes

and, for nothing, gives back whatever light—
sun's, moon's. A bird that is not a gull

passes over; I mark what you would: underneath,
at the tip of either wing, a fluorescent-white

moon, or round star. Does the bird itself
ever see this? According to you *many have*

had the ashes of lovers strewn here,
on this beach on this water that now beats at,

now seems to want just to rest alongside.
The dead can't know we miss them   Presumably,

we were walking   *that we are walking*
upon them.

III.
All night, again,
a wind that failed to bring storm—

instead, the Paradise dream: the abandoned
one nest at a bad angle—in danger,

and what it is to not know it;
the equally abandoned one tree that,

for the time being, holds it—alone,
and what it is to not know it.

All morning, it has been the fog
thinning at last,

as if that were the prayer,
the streets filling with men *as if they*

were divine answer and not just
what happens. Do I love less, if less is

all I remember? Your mouth, like a hole
to fly through. What you understood

of the flesh: how always first are we
struck down. *Then we rise; are astounded.*

The Latin of Section I of "The Blue Castrato" translates: "Lord—as it pleases you—restrain me."

The opening stanza of "On Morals" paraphrases advice given by Sun Tzu toward the end of his chapter "Doing Battle" in *The Art of War*, edited by Thomas Cleary, published by Shambhala Publications, Inc., 1991.

"Renderings" is comprised variously of translations, graftings of translation on my own voice-variations of particular authors, and—in the case of *Anonymous* and *From an Epitaph*—my own interpretations of Greek voices from the seventh century B.C. All translations and portions of translations are my own, from the Greek text of David A. Campbell's *Greek Lyric Poetry*, published by Macmillan, 1976.

The poet in line 12 of "Alba: After" is Eugenio Montale. The statement attributed to him can be found in the last two lines of the untitled section of his *Ossi di seppia*, which begins "Arremba su la strinata proda."

The last five lines of "A Great Noise" are after a description Georgia O'Keeffe gives of her relationship with Alfred Stieglitz in the Metropolitan Museum's catalog, *Georgia O'Keeffe by Alfred Stieglitz*. I thank Jan Garden Castro, in whose book *The Art and Life of Georgia O'Keeffe*, published by Crown Publishers, Inc., 1985, I first read this description.

"Two Versions of the Very Same Story" is after Borges's prose piece "*Inferno, I*, 32," which appears in *Dreamtigers*, translated by Boyer and Morland, published by the University of Texas Press, 1964.

All italicized lines in "The Full Acreage of Mourning" are from the Book of Proverbs, as it appears in *The Old and the New Testaments of The Holy Bible*, Revised Standard Version, Second Edition, published by Thomas Nelson, Inc., 1971.

With the exception of line 7, the final section of "Meditation" (*Isaiah*) is a free arrangement of lines from the Book of Isaiah, as it appears in *The Old and the New Testaments of The Holy Bible*, Revised Standard Version, Second Edition, published by Thomas Nelson, Inc., 1971.

CARL PHILLIPS is the recent recipient of a Guggenheim Fellowship, and the author of two previous poetry collections: *In the Blood*, winner of the Morse Poetry Prize, and *Cortège*, a finalist for both the National Book Critics Circle Award and the Lambda Literary Award for Gay Men's Poetry. He is an associate professor of English, and of African and Afro-American Studies, at Washington University in St. Louis, where he also directs the creative writing program.

The text of *From the Devotions* is set in Otl Aicher's Rotis Serif typeface, designed in the 1980s. Aicher was strongly influenced by the ideals of the Bauhaus, and Rotis is a typographic expression of that movement's attempts to blend technology and aesthetics. Rotis adds distinctly contemporary features to the classic roman letter model.

This book was designed by Will Powers, set in type by Stanton Publication Services, Inc., and manufactured by Bang Printing on acid-free paper.